ISABELLA OF CASTILE
Queen on Horseback

Isabella of Castile
QUEEN ON HORSEBACK

By Joann J. Burch

FRANKLIN WATTS

New York / London / Toronto / Sydney
A First Book / 1991

Cover photographs courtesy of Scala/Art Resource, N.Y. and Historical Pictures Service, Chicago (insert)

Photographs courtesy of: Art Resource, N.Y.: pp. 2, 18, 56 (all Giraudon), 45, 58 (both Scala); Spanish National Tourist Office: p. 9; New York Public Library, Picture Collection: pp. 12, 14; The Bettmann Archive: pp. 16, 23, 29, 36, 38, 49; Earl Dibble: p. 21; Ronald Sheridan/Ancient Art and Architecture Collection: pp. 25, 31; Historical Pictures Service, Chicago: pp. 27, 40, 41, 47; American Numismatic Society: p. 30; Odyssey/Frerck/Chicago: pp. 34, 50, 53.

Library of Congress Cataloging-in-Publication Data

Burch, Joann Johansen.
Isabella of Castile : Queen on horseback / Joann J. Burch.
p.   cm. —(First book)
Includes bibliographical references and index.
Summary: Examines the life and accomplishments of the Spanish queen who brought political and religious unity to her kingdom and made it possible for Columbus to sail west.
ISBN 0-531-20033-7
1. Isabella I, Queen of Spain, 1451–1504—Juvenile literature.
2. Spain—History—Ferdinand and Isabella, 1479–1516—Juvenile literature.   3. Spain—Kings and rulers—Biography—Juvenile literature.   [1. Isabella I, Queen of Spain, 1451–1504.   2. Kings, queens, rulers, etc.]   I. Title.   II. Series.
DP163.B87   1991
946'.03'092—dc20
[B]
91-3173   CIP   AC

CONTENTS

GROWING UP

SIX HUNDRED YEARS AGO, Spain was divided into five kingdoms, each with its own ruler. King John II ruled Castile, the largest of the five kingdoms. He ruled for forty-eight years, but did not care about politics. He was more interested in books, dancing, and art. As a result, Castile was not a strong kingdom.

On April 22, 1451, his daughter, Princess Isabella, was born. Both King John and his wife had hoped for a boy so they could be sure a male heir would become king after John's death. A girl would only be considered for the crown if there were no male heir. King John already had a son, Henry, from an earlier marriage, so he was not very disap-

pointed when the princess arrived. Later another son, Alfonso, was born.

Princess Isabella's first years in the palace were happy ones. But when she was three and a half years old, her father became very ill. Before he died, he asked his son, Prince Henry, to care for Isabella and her baby brother, Alfonso. Henry, who was twenty-nine years old, promised that he would. However, as soon as he was crowned King Henry IV, he banished Isabella, Alfonso, and their mother to the castle she had inherited from King John. He did not want any of them as part of his court.

The castle was a dark, cold, dreary place to live. The stone floors had no carpets to soften footsteps, and the stone walls had no tapestries hanging on them to give warmth. There was not much furniture, and there were not enough candlesticks. The narrow windows let in little light or heat, even in the summer.

Isabella had only one friend, Beatriz de Bobadilla, the daughter of the castle's governor, or keeper, Don Pedro. They were about the same age and enjoyed playing games and exploring the castle. Sometimes they climbed the stone stairs in the tower and watched for the king's messengers galloping up the dusty road. Usually they saw only sheep grazing on the rolling hillsides. A few times

The kingdom of Castile, in the heart of Spain, owes its name to the many castles—castillos— built as fortresses against enemies.

they peeked through the iron gates of the dungeons beneath the castle. The cold, damp smell sent shivers through Isabella.

Isabella and Beatriz also studied together. They went to the village church to learn about their Catholic religion. Priests and tutors came to the castle to teach them reading, grammar, poetry, and history. Isabella's mother taught them manners, needlework, and music. Don Pedro was so grateful for his daughter Beatriz's education that when the two girls were six years old he gave each a pony and taught them to ride.

Riding soon became Isabella's favorite pastime. By the time she was ten, she owned her own horse. In Castile, women and children normally rode mules. But horses went faster than mules, and Isabella loved to race among the rocks and grazing sheep with her hair streaming behind her. She learned to hunt rabbits and deer, and became such an excellent horsewoman other riders could barely keep up with her.

Isabella's mother told her riding fast and hard was not princesslike. She always reminded her daughter that even though her father was dead, she was still the daughter of a king. She taught her to act like a princess. Isabella tried to do what her mother said.

She took tiny steps, as princesses should, except when she was in a hurry. She tried not to raise her voice, but sometimes she forgot. Beatriz helped her remember to keep her clothes neat and her hair brushed.

The year Isabella turned eleven, King Henry ordered her and Alfonso to return to his court. Many nobles were rebelling against him, and because Alfonso was next in line to be king, Henry was afraid the rebels might overthrow him and make Alfonso king. He thought if the children lived at court, he could control them.

The king's palace was very different from the quiet castle. Velvet and tapestries hung on the walls. Thick carpets covered the floors. Henry's wife and the other ladies at court wore gaudy, low-cut dresses, and they painted makeup on their faces and legs. At that time, this was considered to be vain and immoral. Isabella was shocked by what she saw and heard.

Although many people lived at court, Isabella was lonely. The only person she felt comfortable talking to besides her younger brother was her "confessor," Father Tomás de Torquemada. (A confessor is a Catholic priest who listens to people review their sins and helps them try to do better.) Torquemada taught Isabella that she should trust God

Father Tomás de Torquemada was Isabella's confessor.

completely. That meant not to question any of the teachings of the Church, including the belief that Christianity was the true religion.

When Isabella turned thirteen, King Henry began to make marriage plans for her. In the fifteenth century, a princess had to marry the man the king thought would increase his power or bring him more land. Henry decided Isabella should marry the prince of the kingdom of Portugal. He was fat, ugly, and old enough to be her father, and Isabella was able to talk Henry out of the marriage.

But she could not talk him out of the next marriage he planned for her. Henry needed soldiers to defeat the rebels in Castile, so he made a bargain with Pedro Giron, head of a powerful group of Castilian knights. If Giron gave him soldiers, Henry would give him Isabella as a wife.

Isabella cried in the arms of her friend Beatriz, who had moved to King Henry's court. She prayed for three days, asking God to spare her from the marriage. In the meantime, everyone else was preparing for the wedding. Giron set out for Madrid. During the night he became ill with stomach pains, and four days later he died. When Isabella heard the news, she cried with relief and thanked God for answering her prayers.

During the next few years, Henry was too busy

A nineteenth-century artist's picture of what knights and explorers of Isabella's time looked like

to arrange another marriage for Isabella. Rebellious nobles had started a civil war because Henry hadn't kept his promises to be a better ruler. He taxed his subjects heavily and spent the money on luxuries for himself and his court. The rebels planned to make Alfonso king. However, when the boy was fourteen, he became ill and died.

Isabella was now seventeen and heir to the throne of Castile. Marriage proposals poured into the kingdom. The one she liked best was from Prince Ferdinand, heir to the kingdom of Aragon. He was her second cousin, but they had never met.

Aragon bordered Castile on the east and was the second largest Christian kingdom in Spain. If Isabella and Ferdinand married, the two kingdoms could unite to become an important country. Isabella thought Henry would be pleased because this marriage would make Castile more powerful.

But Henry had other ideas. Portugal was a more important kingdom than Aragon. He wanted Isabella to marry the same man she had turned down when she was thirteen. He was now king of Portugal, but he was also five years older and as ugly as ever. Isabella refused.

Henry threatened to have her imprisoned until the wedding. Isabella had to act fast. She pleaded with Archbishop Carillo to help bring about a marriage for her with Ferdinand. Carillo sent a messenger to Aragon to ask Ferdinand to come at once. Then Carillo and Isabella galloped off to a palace in Valladolid where she would be safe from Henry's troops.

Ferdinand did not want to be captured by Hen-

15

Ferdinand of Aragon (1452–1516)

ry's troops on his way to meet Isabella. He dressed in ragged clothes and pretended to be the mule driver and servant for six knights who disguised themselves as merchants. The group stayed off the roads and traveled through sheep pastures so Henry's soldiers wouldn't find them. When they stopped for the night, Ferdinand took care of the mules and waited on the so-called merchants.

Ferdinand arrived at Valladolid on October 15, 1469. Isabella liked the prince immediately. She thought his dark hair, bushy eyebrows, and light brown eyes made him handsome. Although he was short, he was only seventeen and could still grow. He was muscular, athletic, and very self-confident.

Ferdinand may not have found Isabella attractive. Her pale face was round and plain. But she had pretty red hair and eyes that changed from blue to green. Ferdinand was pleased that she would be queen of Castile when Henry died, and as her husband, he would become king of both Castile and Aragon.

When he read the marriage papers, however, Ferdinand learned that although he would be called king in Castile, Isabella would have most of the power. He didn't want the title of king without the power. Isabella promised him they would be equal partners.

17

*Isabella and Ferdinand were to rule as equals.
Isabella promised before they married that
they would share the power of the crown.*

On October 19, 1469, Isabella and Ferdinand were married. They were so poor that they had to borrow money from rich nobles to pay for the expenses of the wedding and the simple celebrations afterward. Normally, a royal wedding was very elaborate and had lavish festivities that lasted for many days. But Isabella didn't care about expensive celebrations. She was happy to be married to the man of her choice.

QUEEN OF CASTILE

ISABELLA WROTE to King Henry about her marriage to Ferdinand, and promised they would be loyal subjects. King Henry was furious and took away her right to be queen as punishment for marrying without his permission. He decided that his nine-year-old daughter, Juana, not Isabella, would be queen of Castile when he died.

The year before, the Cortes, Castile's parliament, had declared Isabella to be the legal heir to the throne. The common people supported her, too. They admired the dignified and moral life she led. They disapproved of Henry because of the way he wasted the kingdom's money. They also did not approve of his immoral court life.

King Henry died in 1474, when Isabella was

20

*In 1474 Isabella set out from
the Alcazar (fortress-palace) of Segovia
to be crowned Queen of Castile.*

twenty-three years old. Isabella declared herself queen of Castile. The next day, in an elaborate ceremony, Archbishop Carillo placed the crown of nine diamonds, seven rubies, and seventy-four pearls on her head. The crowd cheered, bugles blew, bells rang, and castle cannons fired a salute to the new queen of Castile. After the ceremony, Isabella went to the cathedral to pray for a peaceful and prosperous reign.

Ferdinand was in Aragon helping his father fight a war against the French. Isabella wrote to him about Henry's death, and told him he was now king of Castile. As soon as he received her letter, Ferdinand hurried back to Castile. He was angry that Isabella had not waited for him to be crowned with her. She explained she had to claim the throne before King Henry's daughter, Juana, did.

Like most fifteenth-century men, Ferdinand did not believe women should rule a kingdom. Wives were expected to obey their husbands, and he thought he should be in charge of Isabella's kingdom. He felt that she should stay in the palace and raise princes and princesses while he governed Castile.

Isabella had no intention of giving up her right to the throne. First she tried to reason with Ferdinand. If Castile did not let women rule, their daughter Isabella could never be queen. Then she

*The people of Castile cheered
their new queen.*

promised him, "In Castile, your wishes will be law." She also agreed to let Ferdinand's name come before hers on all documents they signed. From that day forward, Isabella referred to Ferdinand as "My lord, the King," an expression of her great respect for him.

Not everyone in Castile wanted Isabella to be queen. The nobles loyal to Henry thought Juana should be queen. Since she was only thirteen years old, they thought they could control her and thereby control Castile. They planned for her to marry Alfonso V, king of Portugal, the same man Henry had chosen for Isabella. King Alfonso wanted revenge for Isabella's earlier rejection of him, and he was eager to become king of Castile. He demanded that Isabella resign the crown in favor of Juana.

Isabella remained calm. She wrote Alfonso, asking him to discuss the situation. He replied by invading Castile with his army of twenty thousand soldiers. This was a catastrophe. The last thing Isabella and Ferdinand wanted was war. They had neither an army nor the money to buy supplies and weapons. All they had was Ferdinand's experience fighting wars in Aragon and Isabella's talent for organizing.

Isabella and Ferdinand spent months on their horses, crisscrossing Castile to recruit soldiers. By July

Queen Isabella's crown

of 1475, forty thousand men had enlisted. While Ferdinand trained the army, Isabella raised money and arranged for supplies. She spoke to town councils and important nobles, asking them to help drive out the Portuguese by giving food, money, and men. She also borrowed money from the Church, which she promised to pay back in three years.

In five months, Castile's army was ready to fight the invaders. Ferdinand marched his troops to the border of Portugal, where Alfonso's army had camped while waiting for reinforcements from Castilian rebels. Isabella stayed forty-four miles (about 70 km) away to supply Ferdinand's soldiers with food and weapons. She also put on armor, rode at the head of her troops, and led the cavalry on raids. Her strategy was to cut off the men and supplies coming for King Alfonso.

On March 1, 1476, Castile won the Battle of Toro, the turning point of the war. The battle was hard fought. When the two armies rushed at one another, horses and men fell in the icy mud. It was so cold that some of the men's armor froze, making it impossible for them to move. After the battle ended, Isabella exclaimed, "My lord, the King, has saved Castile." Isabella did not take credit for the victory, but without her help the battle would not have been won.

Although the war lasted for three more years, only skirmishes, or small fights, erupted. Ferdinand and Isabella divided their troops. Ferdinand traveled through northern Castile, destroying enemy castles used by nobles as strongholds. Isabella moved her headquarters to Seville, in southern Castile. Her advisers were horrified that their queen would continue to put herself in danger, especially since she was pregnant. But she believed her duty as queen was more important than her personal safety.

Young Queen Isabella, a strong and talented ruler, played an important role in the battle against Portugal.

On June 30, 1478, the new male heir to the throne of Castile and Aragon was born. The baby was named John after both grandfathers. The entire kingdom celebrated his birth. Isabella was so happy she allowed a bullfight to take place. She hated this sport, but she knew Castilians loved it.

The war ended the following year. King Alfonso signed a treaty giving up all of his and Juana's rights to the throne of Castile. Juana agreed to leave Castile forever, and moved to Portugal where she became a nun.

With peace in her kingdom, Isabella could reorganize the government. Law and order had broken down during King Henry's twenty-year reign, and the country was ravaged from ten years of war. Isabella wanted to make Castile strong. First, she and Ferdinand set up a police force to rid the kingdom of bandits who murdered and robbed people. Next, they overhauled Castile's money system and built up the treasury. Then they reorganized the Royal Council so that it was no longer controlled by powerful nobles. Lawyers, townsmen, and educated members of the lesser nobility were put in charge. Isabella thought men trained in universities were better able to carry out her reforms.

The Royal Council also became the supreme court of justice. On Fridays, Isabella held sessions for citizens to bring their complaints before her. She vis-

An old engraving shows an artist's
view of a bullfight, a popular
spectacle in Isabella's Castile.

Coins issued during the reign of Isabella and Ferdinand bore the rulers' likeness.

*An old tapestry shows the court
of Ferdinand and Isabella.*

ited at least four towns every year with the Royal Council, and the people in her kingdom grew loyal to her. They saw that she was just and cared about their problems.

Isabella traveled to whatever part of Castile needed her attention. The kingdom had no capital, and the court traveled around the country in caravans of people, animals, and carts. Each of Isabella's five children was born in a different part of her kingdom. The children grew up moving from one end of the kingdom to the other, staying in strange castles, dusty army camps, or beautiful palaces.

Isabella's court was like a schoolroom. She brought outstanding teachers to the court, and insisted that all her ladies-in-waiting learn something: Castilian grammar, another language, history, and so on. She also created a palace school for some of the nobility. Even Isabella studied: she learned Latin at the age of thirty. Rulers and diplomats from other countries spoke to each other in Latin, and Isabella felt uneducated because she knew only the Latin used in the Catholic church.

In six years Isabella accomplished more than any of Castile's kings had done in hundreds of years. And when she had reorganized the government, Isabella turned her energy to another problem: the religious unity of Castile.

CHRISTIANS, JEWS, AND MUSLIMS

CHRISTIANS, JEWS, AND MUSLIMS had lived in harmony in Spain for hundreds of years. Rulers permitted religious differences among their subjects, and people usually accepted these differences. But during the fifteenth century all that changed. Christians rioted against Jews. Muslims in the kingdom of Granada stopped paying tribute, or money, they gave to Castile under an old agreement. They also made border raids into Castile. Isabella was concerned that the government she and Ferdinand had worked so hard to reorganize would be affected by these conflicts.

Most people in Isabella's kingdom were poor Christian farmers. Because of an old law, the Jewish minority was not allowed to own land in Castile. Since they couldn't farm, many Jews worked as

Moors—Muslims from North Africa who had first
moved into Spain in the eighth century—held power
in the kingdom of Granada, south of Castile.

doctors, lawyers, merchants, and bankers. Poor Christians became jealous of the Jews' success and wealth. To make matters worse, when farmers needed a loan, they had to go to Jewish bankers because the Christian religion did not allow its followers to lend money. When people borrowed, they had to pay interest, which was money paid for the privilege of borrowing. Poor farmers resented paying this.

Christians expressed their resentment by rioting against the Jews. Jews feared for their lives, and in order to live safely, some chose to be baptized in the Catholic church. They were called *conversos,* or New Christians. But attacks against them continued because many *conversos* practiced the Jewish religion in secret.

To put an end to this problem, Isabella and Ferdinand set up a special court of inquiry, called an Inquisition. The court would find out which *conversos* were still secret Jews. Isabella's plan was for these false Christians to do penance, acts to show they were sorry for not being true Christians. Once they had done penance, they could rejoin the Catholic church.

The number of cases brought before the courts of inquiry grew so large that Isabella appointed Father Tomás de Torquemada, her old confessor, to

An old engraving shows the Grand Council of the Inquisition examining suspected false Christians.

be in charge of the Inquisition. Christians admired him for his pure life and strong faith. But he caused much human suffering because he was narrow-minded and prejudiced against anyone who was not Christian. He ordered Castilians to report *conversos* they suspected of still practicing the Jewish religion, even if they were friends or relatives.

Suspected false Christians were taken away in the middle of the night. They were tortured until they confessed, even if they had nothing to confess. They were never given a chance to prove their innocence. Hundreds were burned at the stake. Children of victims suffered too, because the family's money was taken away, and the entire family lived in disgrace for the rest of their lives.

Isabella left the Inquisition in the hands of Torquemada because she had other problems in her kingdom. On December 26, 1481, Moors, as the Muslims in Granada were called, attacked Zahara fortress on Castile's southern border. They swarmed over the walls, swinging their curved swords, and killed all the men inside. They then sold the women and children into slavery.

Castile sent spies into Granada to look for a good place to avenge this act of the Muslims. The town of Alhama was chosen, and Ferdinand's army marched in and killed a thousand Moors, throwing their bodies over the city walls for wild dogs to eat. They then cut the chains off hundreds of Christian prisoners kept in dungeons beneath the city.

Isabella and Ferdinand moved their court to Cór-

Those people the Council of the Inquisition judged guilty were tortured or put to death.

doba and set up a war base. While Ferdinand led the troops, Isabella gathered supplies and raised money, as she had done in the war with Portugal. She also established the first military hospital in history. Near the front lines, she installed six tents, complete with beds, medicines, doctors, and nurses. She also provided four hundred covered wagons to be used as ambulances.

Getting supplies to the army was difficult. Southern Castile was mountainous, and there were few roads. Isabella supervised workmen who cut paths through the mountains and built roads and bridges. Pack trains of sixty thousand mules carried food and weapons to the army. Isabella decreed that no woman should ride a mule until the war ended because the army needed animals. The women of Castile helped the war effort by giving up the mules they rode whenever they traveled.

The Moors had built strong forts and city walls to protect themselves from attack, so Ferdinand had to use "modern" weapons such as gunpowder, stone bullets, and bigger cannons. Isabella sent to Germany, France, and Flanders for these weapons. This cost a great deal of money, and she had to pawn her jewels, her gold crown, and precious heirlooms to pay for them.

Both sides stopped fighting during the winter.

The army of Ferdinand and Isabella battled against the Moors in Granada for ten years.

In January 1492, the king of the Moors
surrendered to Isabella and Ferdinand.

When horses and mules sank deep in the mud and the soldiers' metal armor froze, it was necessary to halt the war temporarily. But Isabella didn't want to stop. On November 7, 1490, she battled heavy rain and mountain blizzards on her war horse to visit the battle lines. When Castilian soldiers saw their queen dressed in full armor, they were ready to fight a little longer.

The Granada War dragged on for ten years. By 1491 the only part of their kingdom left to the Moors was their capital, Granada. Isabella and Ferdinand set up colorful tents on the plain outside the city and spent the next year trying to get the Moors to surrender. The army camp grew bigger and bigger as people came from all over Europe to witness the fall of Granada. One of the onlookers was Christopher Columbus.

The Moors finally surrendered, and on January 2, 1492, Ferdinand's army marched to the Alhambra, the most beautiful palace of the Moors. A silver cross was raised on its highest tower. When the royal flag fluttered beside the cross, shouts of joy broke out. "Granada, Granada for King Ferdinand and Queen Isabella," thousands of people cheered. The kingdom of Granada, the last Moorish stronghold in Spain, was now part of Castile.

1492

ONCE THE GRANADA WAR had ended, Isabella could think about other problems in her kingdom. The major problem was the Inquisition. Torquemada believed if Jews were no longer permitted to live in Castile, the Inquisition would end. He told Isabella it was her duty as a good Catholic to not allow any other religion in Castile. He then urged Isabella and Ferdinand to expel all the Jews and false Christians from their kingdom.

On March 30, 1492, Isabella and Ferdinand signed an edict, or law, requiring every Jew in Castile to be baptized into the Catholic church or to leave the kingdom forever. The Jews were stunned. Jewish families had lived in Castile for more than

1,500 years. They had no other home and spoke no language other than Castilian Spanish.

Most Jews prepared to leave rather than become Catholic. When they sold their homes and goods, they received only a small portion of what their possessions were actually worth. Some had to trade a house for a cart or a mule. Others could buy only supplies for the trip.

When the time came to leave, the roads of Castile overflowed. Some of the Jews rode on horses or mules, but most walked. Since they were forbidden to take money out of the kingdom, some of them hid their gold by swallowing it. Many of those who fled to Africa had their stomachs ripped open by Muslims searching for the gold. Most of the Jews went to Portugal. Portugal's King John charged a tax on each person entering his country, but four years later he expelled the Jews from Portugal, even though they had paid the tax.

At the same time that the Jews were leaving Castile, Christopher Columbus was preparing to sail on his famous voyage. Six years earlier, he had gone to Isabella's court in search of money for his trip. He believed he could find a shorter way to the Indies, or eastern Asia. He planned to sail west across the Ocean Sea, as the Atlantic was then called. He felt sure he would discover the land of gold, silk, and

Christopher Columbus, seen here in a fifteenth-century portrait, came to the court of Castile seeking ships and money for a voyage of exploration.

spices, and if Queen Isabella financed the trip, Castile would be rewarded.

Isabella knew she could not afford to pay for this trip until the Granada War ended, but she gave Columbus a small allowance each month so that he would stay in Castile. She didn't want him to go to another country with his idea. She also asked her advisers to study Columbus's project.

Isabella's advisers thought that Columbus's plans were not accurate scientifically. They also did not like the way he bragged and the way he told everyone he was chosen by God to find a new route to the Indies. He also demanded that he be given titles and be made governor of the lands he discovered. And he insisted on 10 percent of all the riches he found in the Indies.

When Castile won the Granada War, Columbus arranged a meeting with Isabella and Ferdinand. He told Isabella the Portuguese were on the verge of discovering a new route to the Indies. A successful trip would bring riches and glory to whatever country got there first. Isabella did not want Portugal to become more powerful, so she gave Columbus what he needed.

Columbus asked for three ships with good crews, along with provisions for two months and goods for trade. Isabella ordered the governor of Palos, a small

*Columbus presented plans for his voyage
to Isabella and her advisers.*

fishing port, to lend Columbus two small ships, the *Niña* and the *Pinta*. A wealthy family of shipowners let him use one of their ships, the *Santa María*. They also helped him recruit a crew of ninety men and boys.

On August 3, 1492, Columbus set sail. Eight months later a messenger delivered a letter to Isabella saying Columbus had returned. Thrilled to hear that he was safe, she commanded him to come to her court at Barcelona.

Columbus received a hero's welcome. Castilians realized his discoveries would make their country powerful, and stood along his route to cheer him. He rode a magnificent horse at the head of a parade. His crew followed, carrying scarlet and green parrots from the Indies. A number of Indians were paraded, wearing gold collars and bracelets, and shivering in the cool air.

In Barcelona, crowds gathered in the plaza outside the cathedral, where the queen and king sat on thrones under a gold canopy. Isabella invited Columbus to sit with them and fifteen-year-old Prince John. They listened closely as he told them about his discoveries and how he had left behind thirty-nine men to start a colony. In truth, they had been left behind because the *Santa María* had been

*Early on August 3, 1492, Columbus took
leave of Isabella and Ferdinand and set sail
in search of a new route to the Indies.*

Isabella welcomed Columbus back to Spain with a great celebration in Barcelona.

wrecked. There was not enough room on the other two ships to take all the men back to Castile.

Isabella was so pleased with Columbus's discovery that she financed three more voyages. When he returned from his third trip, he brought thirty Indians to sell as slaves. Isabella was furious. "What does he think he is doing with my vassals?" she asked, and ordered the Indians returned to their native land on the next trip to the New World. Columbus never found the gold and spices he promised to bring back, but he did discover the continent of America.

ISABELLA'S FINAL YEARS

ISABELLA'S FINAL YEARS were not very happy ones. Prince John, her only son, died in 1497, when he was nineteen years old. Castile had no future king, and the entire kingdom mourned. Isabella was devastated, and for the rest of her life she wore black robes and kept John's dog Bruto at her side. The next year her oldest daughter died after giving birth to a baby boy. The baby became the new heir to Castile, Aragon, and Portugal, but he became ill and died before he was two years old.

In spite of all the sadness in her life, Isabella continued working to make Castile a better kingdom. She also recognized the rights of Indians in the New World, and in her will she noted how important just rule was for them. She continued to travel through-

*A fifteenth-century portrait of Isabella
in her later years*

out Castile, and held court sessions on Fridays for anyone who wanted to bring a problem to her attention.

During the summer of 1504, Isabella and Ferdinand rode to Medina del Campo, near her childhood home, where they both came down with a fever. Ferdinand recovered quickly, but Isabella, who was fifty-three years old, grew worse. She was often too weak to walk, and at times she could not see to write. When she was no longer able to hold a pen, she dictated to her secretaries. Isabella wanted to finish her instructions on how to run the government before she died.

Rumors flew throughout Castile that the queen was dying. Her subjects went on pilgrimages or marched in processions to pray for Isabella's recovery. When she learned of this, she asked her subjects to pray only for the salvation of her soul, not for the health of her body.

Just before noon on November 26, 1504, Queen Isabella died. Ferdinand and Beatriz were at her bedside. All Castile grieved at the loss of the queen they had admired for thirty years, a queen who had dedicated her life to her kingdom and the church.

Isabella's body was taken south to Granada. A funeral procession of nobles and churchmen dressed in black cloaks carried her casket across Castile. During the three-week journey, Isabella's subjects made a last farewell to their queen. Many things, both good and bad, were remembered about Isabella's reign.

The older Castilians remembered the outlaws who had robbed and killed at the beginning of her reign. Some remembered how the Moors in Granada had wanted to conquer Castile. *Conversos* who chose to stay in Castile by joining the Catholic church thought about their Jewish brothers and sisters who had been killed or expelled from the kingdom. Many recalled the fires and torture of the Inquisition. A few onlookers thought about Columbus and wondered if the new lands he had discovered would ever be worthwhile.

The lands Columbus had discovered would indeed turn out to be worthwhile. While he never found the gold and riches he had promised to bring back, they were there. After Columbus died, Spanish adventurers and explorers found fabulous riches in the great Indian empires in Mexico and Peru. Columbus's discovery of the Americas enabled Spain to build a mighty overseas empire which brought the country wealth and power.

When Isabella had become queen in 1474, her kingdom had neither wealth nor power. Castile was a weak, bankrupt kingdom because of the disas-

A fifteenth-century prayer book for Isabella's daughter was illustrated with scenes from the queen's thirty-year reign.

trous twenty-three-year reign of Henry IV. The forty-eight-year reign of Isabella's father, King John II, hadn't been much better. For more than seventy years, the nobles in Castile had competed with the kings for power, wealth, and land. Many nobles were richer than the king. When Isabella needed money to build Castile's army, she borrowed from these wealthy nobles.

Isabella's greatest achievement was restoring the power in Castile to the king and queen. This enabled them to provide their people with good government. Before Isabella's reign, crime and lawlessness had spread throughout the kingdom. King Henry and his corrupt court had set a bad example for the country, and many in the kingdom had become corrupt too. Isabella transformed the kingdom into a peaceful, unified country whose citizens obeyed the law.

Isabella's desire for a unified kingdom had been threatened by the Jewish and Muslim minorities. She sincerely believed that the only true religion was the Catholic faith, and had demanded that everyone in her kingdom be Catholic. But the Spanish Inquisition and the expelling of all Jews and Muslims from the kingdom had been a cruel price to pay for religious unity.

Defeating the Moors in the Granada War had ended centuries of struggle in Spain. Some histori-

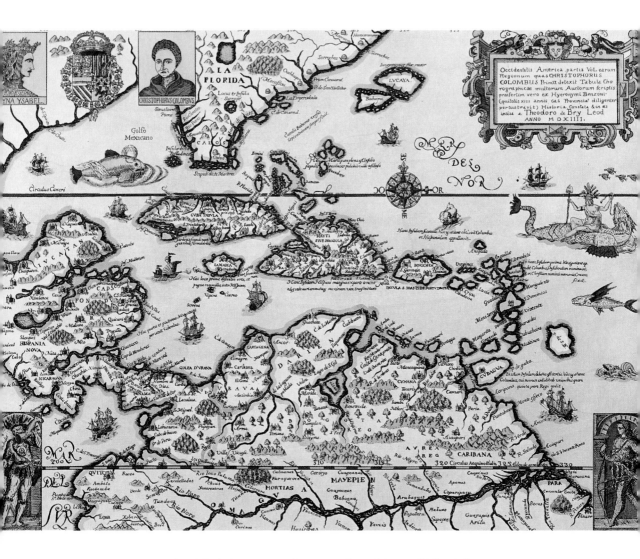

*A 1514 map shows the New World
Columbus discovered while in the service
of Isabella of Castile.*

ans feel this was Isabella's greatest achievement. And as a result of Isabella's victory, Castile became recognized and accepted by the European community as one of the foremost powers in Europe in the sixteenth and seventeenth centuries.

FOR FURTHER READING

Boyd, Mildred. *RULERS IN PETTICOATS.* New York: Criterion Books, 1966.

Davis, Mary Lee. *WOMEN WHO CHANGED HISTORY: FIVE FAMOUS QUEENS OF EUROPE.* Minneapolis: Lerner Publications, 1975.

Farmer, Lydia. *A BOOK OF FAMOUS QUEENS.* New York: T. Y. Crowell Jr. Books, 1964.

Liston, Robert. *WOMEN WHO RULED: CLEOPATRA TO ELIZABETH II.* Englewood Cliffs, N.J.: Julian Messner, 1978.

McKendrick, Melveena. *FERDINAND AND ISABELLA.* New York: Harper & Row, 1968.

Trease, Geoffrey. *SEVEN SOVEREIGN QUEENS.* New York: The Vanguard Press, Inc., 1968.

INDEX